Life Interrupted

Thirty-One Lessons
in
Thirty-One Days

SHAMIKA D. HAMILTON

WESTBOW
PRESS®
A DIVISION OF THOMAS NELSON
& ZONDERVAN

WestBow Press books may be ordered through booksellers or by contacting:

WestBow Press
A Division of Thomas Nelson & Zondervan
1663 Liberty Drive
Bloomington, IN 47403
www.westbowpress.com
1 (866) 928-1240

ISBN: 978-1-9736-7836-6 (sc)
ISBN: 978-1-9736-7838-0 (hc)
ISBN: 978-1-9736-7837-3 (e)

Library of Congress Control Number: 2019917137

Print information available on the last page.

WestBow Press rev. date: 11/20/2019

Contents

Preface

I always knew that I was supposed to write but shrugged it aside. I was too busy to have time to do one of the things I am most passionate about—reaching others through writing what the Lord has laid on my heart. I was so caught up in the whirlwind of life that I hardly had time for it. You know what? I am finally at the place where I realize that this is one of the purposes for which I was born, and I will no longer put it aside. Whatever the Lord puts on my heart, I am definitely going to write, and I know you will enjoy reading it.

We often try to fit into normalcy even when God has a call on our lives that is not. We believe that if we can blend in with the crowd and make ourselves insignificant, God will miss us. God often does drastic things to get our attention and reminds us that even though we might trick the crowd by blending in, He never loses sight of us and the purpose He has prepared for us. God had to shake some things in my life for me to be awakened to the realization that living in my comfort zone was not for me and I was avoiding my purpose.

The Lord has interrupted my life. My plans have now become His plans, and my purpose now has to align with His purpose. *Life Interrupted* is no coincidence. I literally had my life interrupted when I lost my job due to layoffs at work. He used that moment to get my attention and put me on a new path, where I became more committed to His purpose for my life.

> And we know that all things work together for good to those who love God, to those who are the called according to His purpose. (Romans 8:28 NKJV)

May your heart be blessed as I share with you the lessons I have learned and how God's truth is comforting even in the darkest moments.

Be inspired and encouraged, my friends.

Acknowledgments

Thanks be to God, who has made all things possible. Special thanks to my family and friends for your support and encouragement. To those who prayed and continue to pray for me, thank you. To everyone who will come in contact with this devotional, thanks for your support in the work of the Lord. I pray your life will be enriched by this ministry and that your relationship with Jesus Christ will be strengthened.

Introduction

I usually come across books that have been written to inspire us to be great in some area, and that is good. However, I realize that as Christians we are sometimes afraid to get real, especially about areas in our lives where we struggle. We continue to talk about the solutions, but what about the problems—those real struggles and how we have dealt with them and continue to deal with them? So many times I am in the valley, looking for a word of encouragement, trying to find someone who has gone through the same experiences. God's Word is there for guidance and truth; however, I also believe that we must share our experiences so that others can be encouraged and motivated to continue in their walk in the kingdom of God. This devotional is exactly that. It captures the essence of the daily struggles we have as children of God and even the battles we have with God when we can't understand life or when things don't go as planned.

$\mathcal{D}ay$ 1

Lesson: Who or What Is Your Delilah?

Judges 16

Character Profile: Delilah
Nationality: Philistine
Attributes: Pretty, Deceptive, Persistent, Money Loving

Character Profile: Samson
Nationality: Israelite
Attributes: Proud, Inconsistent, Anointed by God

The enemy Philistines knew God had a purpose for Samson, so they used Delilah to stop his purpose. They paid her to betray the secret of his strength. Samson wanted Delilah so badly that even when her deception should have been evident to him, he was oblivious to it. She was persistent, whereas he was inconsistent, and this caused him to miss the mark. He was proud and not strong-willed when it came to the things of God. He was chosen by God and entrusted with this gift, which was to be used for God's glory. He was, however, lax and proud. The account in Judges 16 was the second time he gave in to nagging; he appeared to see himself as self-sufficient. Samson had a character flaw that Satan used against him; where the enemy had been persistent, he was not.

God has a purpose for you too, so the enemy will send something or someone to distract you. Ask God in the name of Jesus Christ to let you see things as they really are through the power of the Holy Spirit, who indwells us and guides us in all truth. The gift of discernment is important in order to separate truth from deception. Like Samson, Satan works through the things we desire the most to bring our downfall (carnal desires). The enemy goes around like a roaring lion, seeking whom he may devour, but be encouraged because greater is He who is within you than he who is in the world.

Day 2

Lesson: The Mind (Desiring God's Will)

So do not throw away this confident trust in the Lord. Remember the great reward it brings you! Patient endurance is what you need now, so that you will continue to do God's will. Then you will receive all that he has promised.
—Hebrews 10:35–36 NLT

How many times have you sat, listened, and thought, *What is it that You require, Lord?* You are torn between the pursuit of your hopes and dreams and wanting to please God. The battle is constant, and you have no break. Within your heart and mind, you feel a deep loyalty to doing God's will, but because of flesh, the battle continues to rage within. You stand, look, and listen, changing your position to see if your mind could just be free. Privately, you say to God, "I want—oh, how I wish—to hear Your audible voice pointing me in the direction I am to take. Oh Lord, please tell me what to do."

It would be so easy if we could always hear God's voice with instructions on which path to take and what blessing we would be given. We would have peace of mind because we would know the outcome. If this were so, we would miss out on some valuable lessons. Each day, there is a battlefield in our minds, but we have the power and authority to stand against the wiles of the devil. God has already equipped us to win the war in our minds and let us shout hallelujah, which is our victory cry. It is a cry that stills the mind and creates an atmosphere for God. When that takes residence, no demons, devils, or vain thoughts can trod.

It is hard to be at a place where you are seeking God and pleading for Him to reveal His will for your life, concerning areas such as school, career, and relationships. Sometimes He seems so far away or silent on the matter. Do not lose courage; it is easy to give up when it seems like nothing is happening. Patience is the key to doing God's will and seeing His promises fulfilled in your life. Let us not rush God but learn from whatever season we are in and trust His guiding hand.

Day 3

Lesson: Courage

For it is by grace you have been saved, through faith—
and this is not from yourselves, it is the gift of God.
—Ephesians 2:8 NIV

How do you find the courage to fight when you feel like you have nothing left within you? You have tried, but one way or another, you just keep messing up. There is a fight outside and within, and you wonder when you will just get it right. The world is watching, tearing you down while they observe, looking for the first opportunity to criticize your fall and actions. You can't control the tears that are flowing, and you wonder, *How, why, and when?* You search within and know you have done wrong, said the wrong things, and acted the wrong way. During all this, you still wish they would see your point. You were defending something you believed in but ended up in the wrong. You don't know the first step from here. "How can I mend what is broken?" is the first question you ask yourself.

You wish you could go back in time, mind your own business, and keep your big mouth shut. (That crosses our minds sometimes.) If only it were that simple. Here you are living with regrets, wishing you could get the moment back. Oh, how you would act differently! Then you think about letting your light shine before others so that they may see your good works and come to glorify your Father in heaven. You messed up once again, and now you are begging again for mercy and forgiveness.

Lord, please forgive me for all the wrongs done.

We have all been at this place, but God is a God of second chances, so even though you might fall, His love urges you to get up.

Have you ever been to that place where you genuinely never meant to hurt someone? You were merely defending a point or taking a stand for what you believed in, but somehow you raised your voice too much, said the wrong thing, or behaved in a way that would make the Lord embarrassed. Usually, if you are a person who listens to the Holy Spirit's conviction, after such incidents, you feel bad. Are you at a place of trying to figure out when you will get it right? Well, God never condemns us when we sin. He actually points out the offensive behavior and offers forgiveness.

It is on us now to acknowledge and repent of these behaviors and practices.

The Word says we should never make a practice of sinning. Some of us feel badly because we question how stuff like that can be in us if we are children of God. Well, that is an area of weakness that God's grace can overcome. The devil wants to keep you condemned, but find the courage to acknowledge your wrongs, confess, and move on. Be empowered and know this: the only power the devil has over you is the amount of access you give him to your life.

> "Submit yourselves, then, to God. Resist the devil
> and he will flee from you" (James 4:7 NIV).

Be encouraged that it's a new second, minute, hour, day, month, and year; you have the opportunity to start fresh right now. It's past and gone. Now go work with Jesus at making things right. God bless you!

Day 4

Lesson: Our Journey

Putting out to sea from there, we encountered
strong headwinds that made it difficult to keep
the ship on course, so we sailed north of Cyprus
between the island and the mainland.
—Acts 27:4 NLT

Our life is a journey that can be contrasted with Paul's journey to Rome in Acts 27. As soon as the brethren headed out to sea, they encountered strong headwinds. It is the same thing with our lives. As soon as we make the decision to accept Jesus Christ as our personal Lord and Savior and start doing His will, it often *seems* like everything that can go wrong starts to go wrong. This is the point when the devil realizes that he has lost the battle for our soul, so he tries to discourage us; hence, we are faced with our strong headwinds.

In Acts 27 (I recommend you read the whole chapter in your quiet time), the headwinds were so strong that they had to take a detour; it was difficult for them to stay on course. It is the same way we often handle the situations and problems in our lives. We take a detour to help ourselves instead of allowing Jesus Christ to guide us through. This is the same Jesus who said, "Peace, be still," to the waves, so He knows and can control the storms in our lives.

Whether it is financial, sexual, marital, or out-of-control children, to name a few, He is able. Let us stay on course and allow God to be the captain in life's storms.

Day 5

Lesson: The Sore Thumb

If the world hates you, keep in
mind that it hated me first.
—John 15:18 NIV

As a child, having a cut, especially in an area that was visible, and going to school could be one of the most uncomfortable situations. This was because it was hard to hide, and children would scorn you. Even those devoted friends you always played with stayed away because they could not be associated with you, or they would risk being teased as well. Do you remember trying as much as you could, within your power, to hide the cut by putting your hands in your pocket or wrapping it under a handkerchief?

To get out of going to school, you told your parents you wanted to stay home until it got better, or you faked sickness. For the lucky ones, this worked, but for others, they were marched right to school.

Sticking out like a sore thumb is not always cool, especially when it makes you the center of cynicism, criticism, and ridicule. Oftentimes, whether at work, school, or our own homes, we are the sore thumb, standing for righteousness in exchange for being unpopular. The Lord Jesus said if the world hated Him, it would hate us too. So are you going to make an excuse to stay away from doing what God has called you to do, or will you wave your "sore thumb," knowing that Jesus Christ is the reason for it? I wish we would all commit to our calling in Jesus Christ and say these words, "I want to be a sore thumb for You, Lord Jesus, even though I may lose friends and family. I know with You the gain will be far greater."

Day 6

Lesson: How Far Can You See?

But without faith it is impossible to please Him, for he who comes to God must believe that He is, and that He is a rewarder of those who diligently seek Him.
—Hebrews 11:6 NKJV

The Lord told Abraham that he was giving him all the land as far as he could see (Genesis 13:14–17). A similar account is found in the book of Joshua. The Lord told Joshua that wherever he set his foot was land he had given to him (Joshua 1:3). The fulfillment of these promises was dependent on the faith of those who received them. Let us learn from the example of the children of Israel. Even though God had given them the Promised Land, when the twelve spies went in to survey it, ten of them forgot God's promises and brought back a bad report (Numbers 13:31). Caleb, like Joshua and Abraham, however, believed God (Numbers 13:30).

Sometimes our sight is limited by the circumstances around us—for example, by what others have to say and by our current situation. If God has given you a vision, do not be afraid to step out in faith, as He will do what was promised. I took a leap of faith in publishing this devotional. I didn't have three-quarters of the resources needed to take on this venture and get the material out there. However, I knew what the Lord had spoken to my heart, and though I was uncertain of what lay ahead, I still decided to move forward. God can only speak the truth because there is no lie in Him. He never promised a smooth journey, but He promised to be with us in everything we do, guiding us safely into all He has prepared for us.

How far is your spiritual sight, which is activated by your faith in God? Once the thing you desire is in God's will for your life, nothing and no one can stop you from accomplishing it but you. Will you trust Him today?

Day 7

Lesson: Making the Right Decisions

Let the peace of Christ rule in your hearts,
since as members of one body you were
called to peace. And be thankful.
—Colossians 3:15 NLT

Once you begin to worry, I am telling you that you have not included God in your plans or turned situations over to Him. God needs you to hear this.

God gives us peace to guide us in the decisions we make, even the hard ones. If we have no peace, then it is not of Him. I also recognize from my own experiences that a lot of times I have decisions to make, and I am the one doing all the talking, and God is there patiently waiting to get a word in. While we need to have the relationship where we tell Him everything, we need to stop and listen to what He is saying. Jesus Christ knows all things and is first place in all things. When we know this, we can trust Him to guide our decisions. He has given us the Holy Spirit, who is there to guide us into all truth. In Jesus Christ are all hidden treasures of wisdom and knowledge. We must clothe ourselves with the things of God and stop and listen to what He is saying. Then we should evaluate the paths before us, using His revelations to move forward. Pray right now that God will fill you with His will, knowledge, and understanding through the Holy Spirit to ensure the right, not favorable, decisions are made.

Week 1

Action Plan

Identify the areas in your life that you
need to work on in accordance with the
material that was covered in week 1.
This is necessary as you advance
in the kingdom of God.

Day 8

Lesson: Don't Give Up

"Timothy, my son, here are my instructions for you,
based on the prophetic words spoken about you earlier.
May they help you fight well in the Lord's battles."
—1 Timothy 1:18 NIV

Faith is the catalyst for change, and a lack of it will prevent the promises of God from being fulfilled in your life. The weakness of faith suggests that you are not fully able to trust God with all areas of your life. Little or no belief prevented the children of Israel, the generation that came out of Egypt, from entering the rest that God had promised them, as is seen in Hebrews 4:1–5.

Has God prophesied over your life, and have you failed to believe Him? Does what seems like His slow timing in your eyes, but which is perfect timing according to His will, cause you to give up? God hears your concerns, and He hears you asking Him when your time for that breakthrough will be. Today, I remind you that your prayers carry much weight in heaven and are not falling on deaf ears. Nor are they insignificant, contrary to what the enemy wants you to believe. Even when it seems like nothing is happening, God is working behind the scenes. Continue to hold on to everything God has prophesied over your life. It shall come to pass. I encourage you to really recommit to what the Lord has declared over your life. Rekindle that flame of hope. As the enemy repeats doubt, fear, and impatience, I urge you to stand on God's Word (Genesis 18:14). As Paul encouraged Timothy in 1 Timothy 1:18, I encourage you today to stand firm because the Lord's Word will be fulfilled, and nothing and no one can stop it unless *you* allow it. Your biggest hindrance is you, so lift your faith!

Day 9

Lesson: Once Is All It Takes

Numbers 20

The Lord told Moses to speak to the rock, but instead he struck the rock. Moses might have done it out of frustration, and God would have been willing to overlook that if that was the case, as He understands human nature. However, God saw something greater. He saw that the underlying cause was lack of faith. A lack of faith in God led to Moses's disobedience. This one action led to him missing out on the blessing of the Promised Land.

We have access to the grace of God; however, sin creates open doors in our lives. The Lord warned Cain that sin was crouching at his door, but he did not listen (Genesis 4:7). The enemy is waiting for an opportunity to sift us as wheat (Luke 22:31). A lack of faith can lead to disobedience, and all it takes is one opening for the enemy to derail us and wreck our lives. From my experiences, when we drift from God, it takes a whole lot of effort to get back on track. It is the Holy Spirit who draws us, but we also have to make a conscious effort to walk in alignment with God at all times.

One action changed Moses's destiny, as he was the person who should have led the children of Israel into the Promised Land. However, Joshua was given that mandate instead. Set a quiet time with God to really reflect on the passage found in Numbers 20 and ask how this applies to you today.

Day 10

Lesson: God's Promises Are True

His divine power has given us everything we need
for a godly life through our knowledge of him
who called us by his own glory and goodness.
Through these he has given us his very great and
precious promises, so that through them you may
participate in the divine nature, having escaped the
corruption in the world caused by evil desires.
—2 Peter 1:3–4 NIV

The twelve spies were sent into Canaan to scout out the Promised Land. Caleb was one of the two who brought back a favorable report about the land, and because of this, God promised him an inheritance. At age eighty-five, he went to Joshua, Israel's leader at the time, with confidence, ready to possess his inheritance. Can you imagine? Caleb, at age eighty-five, was raring and ready to go out and possess all that God had promised him. His body might have been aging, but this spiritual man was strengthened by who had made the promise. God is trustworthy, and Caleb knew that once He was with him, nothing could stand in the way of the promise being fulfilled. Caleb had waited on God for the opportune time for the fulfillment of the promise. Isaiah 40:31 reminds us that those who wait on the Lord, their strength shall be renewed. This is not only a physical but also a spiritual renewal. Be reminded that God is always faithful, so trust Him wherever you are today, as the promise will be fulfilled.

Day 11

Lesson: The Upright Shall Have Good Things

For the Lord God is a sun and shield; the Lord bestows favor and honor; no good thing does he withhold from those whose walk is blameless.

—Psalm 84:11 NIV

God will not withhold any good thing from those who walk upright. We might interpret this to mean that whatever we want we will get, as long as we obey God's commands and statues. However, my question is this: would you want the things that are not His will for your life because you thought them good?

In light of this statement, the first thing we have to recognize is the character of God—who He is, what He represents, and how much He cares. The Word of God says that while we were yet sinners, Jesus Christ died for us. What an awesome love. God's character embodies love, and if something is not good for you, but you think it is, He will not give it to you. You might nag until He gives it, but is that what you really want? Does the thing you desire glorify God? Will it cause a rift in your relationship with Him? How many times do you get mad at God because He said no or wait? But know this: God knows best and will give only the best to you. So if He denies your request, it was never good for you in the first place, or the timing may not be right. My friend Levine once said that "sometimes we are asking God for a stone, thinking it is bread, or we are actually asking for a serpent, thinking it is fish." I had to laugh when she said it because I know I am guilty and the statement is truly profound. It really opened my eyes. Trust God's judgment and know that the child of a king gets only the finest things in life.

Day 12

Lesson: You Never Showed Up

Matthew 22:1–6

God often prepares fellowship meals for us. He is always ready to fellowship with His children. This idea was established from creation when He usually met Adam and Eve in the garden (Genesis 3:8). So many times, He invites us to fellowship, but we are too busy with the cares of life to show up. We spend so much time in pursuit of our dreams, careers, and family. While it is very good to have goals, should those things be most important in our lives? If only we had shown up for fellowship with God. Some of the very things we spend our time acquiring and trying to get are perfectly packaged for us by God, but because we never keep our appointment for that time with God, we cannot receive them. We also expend effort that is not necessary. Are you getting the picture? For many of us, God had to put the package back on the shelf, where it is still today, gathering dust, because we still have not found the time for Him.

Some of the very things you are busy chasing will never be attained outside of a relationship and fellowship with God. There are so many benefits to be had from spending time with God. We keep complaining that we are not hearing from God, but we have to spend time in His presence to train our ears, mind, and heart to hear Him. I find that when I spend time with Jesus Christ, I am not burned out. My day goes better even if situations are unfavorable. I have peace, regardless of what is happening, and I have increased confidence that He is with me, guiding me along the way. The Holy Spirit desires fellowship, but we reject Him so many times. Read and meditate on Matthew 6:33, and I hope we will get it right!

Day 13

Lesson: Seasons

From the tribe of Issachar, there were 200 leaders of the tribe with their relatives. All these men understood the signs of the times and knew the best course for Israel to take.
—1 Chronicles 12:32 NLT

We have four seasons as implemented in creation by God. These are autumn, spring, summer, and winter. In life, we dress, make purchases, and visit certain places according to the season. Each season is marked by various attributes and activities. For people in marketing, it is quite important to know the different seasons so that the marketing campaigns can be tailored accordingly, and it is the same for farmers, who need to know what crops to plant and when to plant them. For these people, the inability to decipher the seasons would mean a disaster in their careers or activities.

As it is in the physical so it is in the spiritual. As Christians, we have to know the season we are in and prepare accordingly. There are times when God says wait, and then there are times He moves and does so quickly. I had been writing since 2015, and I patiently waited on Him for each word to share with you. God knows that by nature I am impatient, always moving at a fast pace, and I believe this was deliberate on His part. He was using that season to help me to grow in this area. I am still a work in progress. I can tell you though that when He decided that it was time to publish this devotional, He did it so quickly. Trust is key as we move through the different seasons we are in. Jesus knew when to step back and when to move forward because He trusted His Father.

We must know God personally because the enemy often disguises himself as an angel of light in the form of opportunities and open doors. Also, he is the master of lies and will seek ways to delay our progress when God has presented opportunities and open doors. What has God said about your life? Do not run ahead of Him and do not be paralyzed by fear if God is telling you to move forward.

I must highlight that whatever season we are in, if we are prepared, we will not be discontented but rather content. Sometimes it seems as if life is happening for everyone else, and you are left behind, asking God when your season of overflow will happen. I am going to reiterate throughout this devotional that your prayers have power, and they are heard in heaven. Continue to be persistent in prayer as you seek God for direction about the season you are in. Pray without ceasing. By doing this, you shut the enemy out. I am not telling you something I have not experienced. Check your life and see the season you are in. There may be some fields to be plowed or watered, or weeds, thorns, and thistles to be uprooted. Let us do it so that when the day of harvest comes, we will not be disappointed in the fruit we see.

Day 14

Lesson: Your Place of Failure, Your Place of Triumph

Luke 5:1–11

I was employed and lost my job due to layoffs, as the organization was under new management and my position was no longer relevant. This led me to start writing and blogging. I was figuring out life, and then something happened: the new company called me back to work. I was called back to work and placed in a totally different position than I had been before, and I had to start all over again. At first, I grappled with the idea of going back. I expressed the struggle in my heart to God and also shared it with several of my close friends. While I was sharing with one of them, she quietly reminded me of something I had shared with her months before from Luke 5. Little did I know that the story I had shared, along with its revelations, would now be used back on me.

In the story, the disciples, being fishermen at the time, were busy washing their nets and probably contemplating their disappointment after they had toiled all night and caught nothing. This must have been really hard, as this was their livelihood. For those people who have spouses and children, it would be difficult to go to work and then come home and tell your family you received no salary. This is a picture of how these guys probably felt, having to go home with nothing.

While they were washing their nets, Jesus stepped into the boat without them even realizing, until He asked Peter to push the boat a little from the shore. I believe it is significant and can be compared to Jesus Christ showing up in our situation, but because we are so busy focusing on the failure, we do not realize immediately that He is there. Jesus stepping in created an opening to change their situation. It is the same with me receiving the call to go back to work. It created another opportunity for God's glory to be seen through me. Having spent an entire night, probably getting little or no sleep and still coming up empty-handed, they must have felt truly exhausted, frustrated, distracted, and disappointed.

In spite of this, Jesus Christ asked Peter and the others to do something, to test their obedience. He asked them to cast down the nets once again. He wanted to test what was in their hearts.

It took great humility and obedience for them to do this once again. I have learned obedience and humility too in going back to work and starting all over again. Jesus Christ knew from the very foundation of the earth that fishing was not the purpose for Peter and the others. They were created to be apostles, and He knew this. Jesus Christ also knew that where they were headed required humility, obedience, and faith, so He used this example to build these characteristics in them. Where you are now is not necessarily the purpose He created you for, but it is a purpose within your very purpose, to get you to where He can fully use you. He reminds us not to despise small beginnings. Joseph was in the luxury of his father's house; then he lost it all when he was sold as a slave by his own brothers. How awful he must have felt to move from comfort to discomfort. However, it was being in slavery that ensured that he fulfilled his purpose of saving Israel and other nations in the time of famine. All things truly work together for the good of those who love the Lord and are called according to His purpose. God has to prepare us for where He is taking us, but we have to act in obedience, casting down our nets again even when we feel ridiculous or frustrated like the disciples.

He urged the disciples to launch out into the deep and let down their net. So it is the same with us. He not only wants us to go back to our place of failure, but in doing so, He is asking us to take a big risk. God wants us to go back to the place of failure, and He wants great faith to be exercised. It is the place of failure because the disappointment was great, but this occurred so that the triumph would be even greater. So there I was going back to the place where I lost my job, to work again, starting all over. I was willing to be obedient and humble while watching God's plans for my life unfold. Once we are sure it is God giving a directive, we have to get past what people will think and say and just do what He says. Even though the disciples had toiled all night and caught nothing, which Peter made sure he told Jesus, he also said at His word he would let down the net again. The disciples obeyed, and they experienced the abundant blessings of trusting and listening to the voice of God. They caught so many fish that the net could not contain the catch. It is in the place of testing that you will find your blessing. Like the disciples, it is the hardest thing to go back to your place of failure. But are you willing to go back so that God can bless you?

Week 2
Action Plan

Identify the areas in your life that you
need to work on in accordance with the
material that was covered in week 2.
Continue to press into all that God has for you.

Day 15

Lesson: Relationships

Love the Lord your God with all your heart and
with all your soul and with all your strength.
—Deuteronomy 6:5 NIV

Have you ever had a good thing going with God, and as soon as you commit yourself to a relationship with a man or woman, your relationship with God starts to deteriorate? That probably means that you have a tendency to start putting that person in God's place. You get so caught up in that relationship with that person, talking long hours, going out, and so on, and when it's time for God, you are exhausted. It is important to wait on God and also know that He wants to teach you how to create a balance. Have you ever wondered why your relationships don't work? It is not that God does not want you to get married, but you are compromising your relationship with Him. God has been trying to teach you all along that you have to put Him first and not compromise your relationship with Him because if you do, your relationships with others will never work, as He is the source. A good source is reliable and authentic, and that is just who our God is.

I had this experience when I started dating. Everything started out great, and God was at the center, in control. I then started to slowly drift because my relationship was being placed on a pedestal, taking the place of God in my life. I was so caught up that I found it difficult to make time for prayer, the Word, or sitting with Jesus. This was all on me because the person I was dating was not pressuring me for anything. I was smitten and thought that it was one of the best things to happen. I was no longer single. We have to be careful that nothing and no one takes the place of God. Our relationship with Him must be first because everything that is placed before Him becomes an idol. Little by little, the relationship with the person I was dating started to unravel, and I knew exactly what was happening. I needed no one to tell me because I already knew. I had given this relationship first place, the place of God, and God does not play second fiddle. It had to fall apart because He was no longer included. I actually bumped Him out. At that point, I had to repent and give everything to God and let Him have His rightful place. Always give God His rightful place in your life so that He can guide your relationships.

Day 16

Lesson: Trials

John 16:33 and James 1:2–3

I don't like to hear the word "trials" because all I usually think about is the accompanying testing and suffering. I would selectively read passages in the Bible or devotionals because I just did not want to read about trials. I did not want any. I would feel such unease, and occasionally I still do when it comes to that word. It is amazing though that God is able to change our perspective through His Word about that word. Trials present an opportunity for growth, a closer walk with God, and they produce spiritual blessings. It is often through trials that we are able to offer the greatest service within God's kingdom. It provides an opportunity to edify others and even shows us that we are more than the limitations we have placed on ourselves. It also gives us a heavenly and healthy perspective, as we see ourselves in the true light that God sees us. There are things that have happened in my life that I did not know I could endure, but through God's grace, I came out as pure gold.

Let us not ask God to make our lives easier but rather to strengthen us to face trials and every new day. We desire God's favor, so we often ask for it so that we don't have to work as hard as we do for certain things. While that is a privilege of being a child of God, trials are there to propel us into God's plan for our lives. Let us ask for the grace to handle whatever we might face and the strength to persevere. If we shall do greater works than Jesus Christ, then we will also have greater trials. Think of trials as your birthing period and the joy that will be experienced thereafter. I know some of you might say, "I have been through trials, and right now I am not experiencing joy." That is okay. If you allow the Holy Spirit to have His way, your joy will come (Psalm 30:5 and Isaiah 61:3). That is why joy is not born out of flesh but is the work of the Holy Spirit. Your trials will most definitely get you to your destiny.

Day 17

Lesson: Why Have You Been Seeking God?

Remember how the Lord your God led you all the
way in the wilderness these forty years, to humble
and test you in order to know what was in your heart,
whether or not you would keep his commands.
—Deuteronomy 8:2 NIV

We often seek God for our own personal gratification or because of a hidden motive. God told Israel that He caused them to wander in the desert, so He could test what was in their hearts. We often seek God because we are looking for solutions to make our lives easier—the desire being driven by me, myself, and I, that famous trio. Let us start seeking God because we desire to know Him better. Let it be driven by a desire to know the scriptures better, to gain new insights and revelations. We might want to know why He said something or why an event occurred in the Word. Seek God to edify yourself so that you can edify someone else and to strengthen your spiritual armory.

We have to do so to ensure that we, or His body, do not become spiritually malnourished. Let us seek Him with the motive of discovering or rediscovering our true purpose in His kingdom. We seek God to know the truth so that when the father of lies presents his case, we are able to stand. I worked as a bank teller, and in banking, we are trained to know the authentic currency so that we can easily identify the counterfeit. We must know the truth so that we can stand. Paul reminds us that our battle is not with flesh and blood enemies but unseen forces that want to destroy us. The Bible explicitly states that Satan and his agents are defeated, but he does not accept this.

We must seek God with the right motives to ensure we are covered at all times. So the next time the question of seeking God is raised in your mind, seek Him out of curiosity to know Him better.

Day 18

Lesson: The Test of Love

Love is patient, love is kind. It does not envy, it does not boast, it is not proud. It does not dishonor others, it is not self-seeking, it is not easily angered, it keeps no record of wrongs. Love does not delight in evil but rejoices with the truth. It always protects, always trusts, always hopes, always perseveres.

—1 Corinthians 13:4–7 NIV

Examinations at times come with a theory and practical section to prove whether or not learning has taken place. The key to being successful is adequate preparation. During the different seasons of life, we spend time in the Word of God, and that is known as the theory. But then comes the time for application, known also as the practical section. The practical shows whether or not you are ready for the blessing or the test. As it relates to marriage, until you are ready to accept your partner with all of their faults and put aside certain expectations, you are not ready for the true depiction of marriage, which mirrors Jesus Christ's relationship with His church. ("Wow, Shamika, that is such as strong statement because I see people get married, and God uses the relationship as their training ground.") While that is true that God at times uses marriages as a training ground for spiritual growth (all things work together for good), the statement was made so that we can be conscious of what we are committing to when we enter into marriage.

What we do in a relationship should not be dependent on how the other party behaves. If God took that stand, then we would have been cut off from Him already. How you respond may seem stupid and ridiculous, but if it is according to the theory of God's Word, then you are excelling in the practical. God will tell you how to treat others, especially your partner, through His Word. He will also allow situations to happen to show if you are ready and if you have learned. Always remember this and you will not go wrong. Ask God to build a better you while He works on your partner, building a better him/her. You will find the right, not perfect, person, so continue to have a dialogue with God to make it work.

Day 19

Lesson: The Wind of Problems (He Knows)

Your eyes saw my unformed body; all the
days ordained for me were written in your
book before one of them came to be.
—Psalm 139:16 NIV

Have you ever tried walking against the wind on a really windy day? The more you head in the direction of the wind, the more it forces you in the opposite direction. When this happens, I feel as if I am going to be blown away. I even turn to God, wherever I am, and ask Him to turn the wind down a little so that I can walk. I believe it is the same thing with our lives. The more we are faced with problems and try to solve them on our own and in our own strength, the more they seem to spiral into something bigger and overwhelming. Just like the wind pushing us farther away from our desired path, so do problems that we face each day. In this situation, there is a decision to be made. We can speak to God about it and trust Him enough to work it out, or we can continue to struggle against the things we will never be able to change on our own. I believe that all of us should seek His will above everything else in our lives. Once we seek God about everything we do, such as talking to Him about the most minuscule details in our lives, consulting Him before making decisions and basically putting everything to Him, we need not worry—even when problems surface.

If we include God in all areas of our lives, when everything starts to go the opposite of what we expect and all seems to be crashing around us, we can totally trust Him. We need not struggle against the wind of problems in our lives since He knows everything that happens to us, as is illustrated in one of my favorite scripture verses, Psalm 139:16. Remember—God is sovereign, and He made the wind, so He knows how to control it. He made you too, so He knows how to deal with everything you face. Will you put everything to Him today and trust Him to work out every detail of your life?

Day 20

Lesson: God's Will but Your Way

The LORD says, "I will guide you along
the best pathway for your life. I will
advise you and watch over you."
—Psalm 32:8 NLT

It's funny how as soon as we are able to understand life, we start planning it. We are quite careful about how we outline its details—who we will marry, by what age we will marry, how many children we will have or will not have, the career we will choose, and even the car we will drive. As life happens, reality sets in, the wind is blown out of our sails, and the rug is pulled from beneath our feet as we realize that we are aging and these dreams that we have held dear for years have somehow not manifested into reality. (Could it be that this was never God's plan? Is that why this has not happened?)

What is even more amazing is that for those of us who are Christians, we often pray that we want God's will for our lives, yet we plan it meticulously, as shown earlier. I had to be honest with myself recently. I had to be real with God. I wanted His will but on my terms because I wanted all those things for my life that I had dreamed of as a child. "Was that so wrong?" I asked myself. No, it is not. It means I am not fully surrendered to God.

"Why does God's will seem so hard?" I ask myself. I think there is some reservation born out of a mind-set that God's will might place me in situations where I might have to suffer a lot, where I will not get some of the very things I desire, such as the husband, kids, and booming career. I even went as far as to ask God why it seemed like some people get it all, while others have to suffer. One person will choose His will and get all they have dreamed of, and another will choose His will and suffer continuously. I did not want to run the risk of being the person who chose His will and had to suffer. I was stuck in a place where it was God's will but on my terms because I wanted the best of both worlds.

As I write, I realize that the character of God and His Word settle all fears or reservation. Some will seem to be okay and some will suffer because all work together for our good and God's glory (Romans 8:28). It's a privilege to suffer for Jesus Christ (James 1:2). Questions I've asked myself include, Would God withhold something from me if it was good (Psalm 84:11 and Mathew 7:11)?

Does God not love me with an everlasting love (Jeremiah 31:3)? I had to be honest with myself because I knew that I was not fully surrendered.

I decided to pray this prayer: Lord Jesus, You know my heart; please help me to surrender my life totally to You. I want Your will, Lord Jesus. No reservations! I am ready to put me aside.

I know wherever God's will takes me is the best path for my life. I don't know what is to come, but I am choosing to trust Him. (I know this is not easy, but it is doable.)

Day 21

Lesson: The but God Moment

Now faith is confidence in what we hope for
and assurance about what we do not see.
—Hebrews 11:1 NIV

Life is full of people telling us to look at the logic of a situation and that we should be realistic. However, faith always creates that *but God* moment. This is when we operate in the realm the Lord wants us to. When we do this, the words realistic and logical become nonexistent. I remember being employed on a contractual basis at a particular organization, and my coworkers (all with good intentions, of course) told me that it would take three years for me to be removed from this contractual role and given a permanent one because, in reality and logically, that was the company's policy, and they all went through it. I remember them telling me that, but I also remember me not accepting that. I had purposed in my heart that God can do anything, so I spoke to Him about it. I made God an offer He could not resist. I offered Him my faith, and I knew He could do anything. His Word says that without faith, it is impossible to please God, and anyone who comes to Him must believe that He is God and the rewarder of those who diligently seek Him (Hebrews 11:6). I had my *but God* moment when, after a year and a half, I was given a permanent role that was also a promotion. I urge you today to take the limits off of God. This saying is not a cliché; it is real. Do we really understand the awesomeness of the God we serve?

Reality: Joseph, I know we are engaged, but I am pregnant, and I didn't have sex with anyone.

Logic: In order for conception to take place, there must be sexual intercourse between a man and woman.

But God Moment: But the Holy Spirit came upon Mary, and she conceived.

(See Luke 1 and Matthew 1).

Reality: Sarah, you are way past child-bearing years, and, Abraham, you are almost a hundred years old. How are you guys going to conceive?

Logic: Maybe you can adopt. Better yet, use Hagar to bear the child!

But God Moment: But God kept his promise. When Sarah's womb was as good as dead and Abraham was really old, they bore the promised child, Isaac.
(Read Genesis 21.)

Reality: Moses, seriously, how are we going to cross this Red Sea? Pharaoh is behind us, and there are mountains on either side.

Logic: It is best if we return to being slaves and surrender. That way, we will ensure that we do not drown.

But God Moment: But God caused the wind to create a part through the Red Sea, and the Israelites crossed over on dry land.
(Read Exodus 14.)

Reality: This giant called Goliath is really big and strong. His armor and weaponry are so sophisticated.

Logic: How can a young boy take on a giant with some stones and a sling?

But God Moment: But God had been honing David's skill as a young shepherd boy, and His Spirit was on David. David killed Goliath with a single stone.
(Read 1 Samuel 17.)

Let me tell you this: Satan wants to keep us all ensnared and far from the truth, but I tell you that with God, all things are possible. Being logical and realistic has its place, but God uses the foolish things of this world to confound the wise. Believe whatever God has told you because it shall come to pass.

Week 3

Action Plan

Identify the areas in your life that you
need to work on in accordance with the
material that was covered in week 3.
God has beautiful plans for your life.
Your story is coming together!

Day 22

Lesson: Love beyond Expectations

And now abide faith, hope, love, these
three; but the greatest of these is love.
—Corinthians 13:13 NKJV

In relationships, when courting or already married, we have the tendency of keeping record of who said and continues to say the words "I love you" first. For the ladies, most times we hope the man we are courting or married to will tell us first, but have we even considered that they may be feeling the same way? Based on traditions, we all have this bias when it comes to our expectations and gender. We expect the wife to do most if not all the household chores while taking care of the children, and the husband is expected to do jobs around the yard while being the bread winner and the head of the household. I was lying down one day when this thought came to me: Jesus loved us without expectations because He saw who we were and knew that on our own we could not measure up. He was willing to say, "I love you," first, before this very world began. In Psalm 139, He declares how His watchful eyes were always on us. He further declares that He loves us with an everlasting love, and while we were yet sinners, Christ died for us. The Word of God says few people would die for a righteous man, but how many would die for a wicked person? You and I were very wicked, yet Christ died for us without even having a second thought about it, and the greater revelation is that we were doing our own thing, not caring one bit about Him.

We cannot experience true love or even understand it, much less reciprocate it, until we have experienced and understood the love of God. God's love is so pure that it chooses to see the best in us even at our worst. How often have we stopped to see the best in others even at their worst? This is why Jesus Christ could leave the luxury of heaven to come to earth to redeem us. This is why Jesus could easily sit with Mary Magdalene, Zacchaeus, and many others who were so sinful they should have been written off a long time ago.

It is always nice to hear someone say, "I love you," but it is more than an expression; it is a replication of Jesus Christ in action. So when we become so hung up on seeking to hear those words, what are we really trying to accomplish? Are we feeding our emotions, or are we really seeking to experience the love that

Jesus Christ talked about and lived? We must first understand and experience God's love, which is genuine. Then we will not just settle for anything. What I am getting at is that Jesus Christ not only expressed in words that He loves us, He also lived it daily. Let us accept no partner in our lives who will only say those three words and then do nothing else. I might ruffle some feathers here, but can someone outside of Jesus Christ truly love? You have to know Jesus Christ in order to experience love and show love. Let us get past these emotional feelings because only God can help us to live the love He himself gives. Jesus Christ is the source and author of love, and until we open our heart to Him, we will never be truly empowered to love without bias.

If a spouse cheats, how can we truly forgive without Jesus Christ? How can we not keep record of wrongs or injustices done to us without Him? How can we not be easily angered or irritated when our spouse, family, friends or coworkers continue to practice the very thing we keep talking to them about that is wrong? And the list goes on. Apart from God, we can do absolutely nothing. People might argue that those who have accepted Jesus Christ as Lord and Savior still do not love like He does. And they are right; those people are still living in ignorance even though they have received light. Jesus will establish himself in a willing heart. This is where He reveals His truths to a surrendered heart. I am writing this, and I realize that we have all been settling when there is so much to experience in God. The old proverb says that we live what we learn. The reason we are not able to love others as the Word of God states is because we are still ignorant of the Word of God. We might say that no one is perfect, so we can't live the Word of God all the time. But I will say to us that Jesus Christ did it all the time while He was on earth. We might argue further that He was God. Guess what? We were created in His image and likeness. We have been settling for less than the experiences we should be having, settling for less than the good things God prepared for us before the foundation of this world.

Can we know or understand love until we have truly met and understood Jesus Christ? Remember—God was the first to say, "I love you," regardless of who we were and whether or not we said it in return or lived it. This illustrates that His love was pure. If you truly love someone, you are not afraid to say it and live it. His Word says perfect love casts out fear. Some of us are afraid to express love because we believe the other person might not feel the same way, or we are putting ourselves out there. God puts Himself out there each and every day, and some of us continue to ignore Him and refuse Him, but it does not stop Him. If we truly love, it is not dependent on what others do or if they say it and live it in return. Only God can help us to make this possible. If I love you nothing changes that, not even your actions. Love without expectations.

Day 23

Lesson: First Place Always

Do not worship any other god, for the LORD,
whose name is Jealous, is a jealous God.
—Exodus 34:14 NIV

I sat reflecting one morning during my devotion, which is my quiet time with God. I was really bothered that I was not spending enough time with God, in His Word and talking to Him, as I had in the past. It then dawned on me that we often neglect God. The human tendency is that whenever we want things from God, we are in His face constantly, and once we receive what we have been asking for, we become consumed by that very thing. We usually begin to shortchange God. Please note that it is not always the case for everyone, but some people do. Then we wonder why God takes so long to give us what we keep praying for. It clearly shows that we are not mature enough to handle certain blessings at certain stages of our lives. In essence, God is saving us from ourselves.

On the other hand, when we pray and God answers, He knows that we are mature enough to handle whatever it is, but sometimes we still do not exercise this maturity. So, yes, the Lord will bless us when He sees fit, even though sometimes others might feel we are not ready. The Lord knows all things, and it is for us to get it right. He never asks or gives to us what we cannot handle, at times we do not see that it is in us to manage what He has entrusted to us. God has blessed us immensely, so let us start using what He has given us the way He intended it to be used. The blessings should never take the place of God in our lives.

Prayer: Lord, I thank You for Your mercies. Even though You have the power to remove Your blessings, You often do not exercise that power because of Your love and patience toward me. Help me to give You first place always, and may I enjoy Your blessings without compromising my relationship with You.

Day 24

Lesson: Let God

Unless the Lord builds the house, they labor in vain who build it; unless the Lord guards the city, the watchman stays awake in vain.
—Psalm 127:1 NKJV

I often sit and reflect on how the most stubborn, disobedient, and strong-willed of all God's creation are humans. Have we thought about how much easier life would be, especially in the midst of trials, if we just *let God*?

We have many choices as we navigate this path called life. We can choose to include and trust God sometimes, not at all, or at all times. Having gone through a series of trials that I thought would derail me, I realize that God has to be included all the time in order for our affairs to work out and come full circle. Let me backtrack. I had an awesome relationship with God. Our relationship was so intimate that His Word guided my actions, there was quiet time in prayer for me to talk and listen to Him, I studied the Word and did morning devotions, and reactions and decisions were guided by Him. After a while though, everything else started to have preeminence over our relationship. Little by little, I started to make decisions on my own, praying and reading the Word when I felt like it, as these things had now become secondary to the many things in my life that were competing for my attention. I know many reading this have gone through the very same things. As humans, we are different yet similar (this similarity is even more evident as we are grafted in God's family), and the devil knows this, as he has studied us carefully and continues to do so. This is why whenever we experience victory in any area of our lives, especially where we have a weakness, we *must* continue to remain vigilant. Also be mindful that the enemy has no new strategies. He has used the same strategies throughout time to ensnare us. We keep giving him access to our lives by failing to follow the instructions that God has given us, which are stated in His Word. In essence, we often create the door and keep it open, which is an invitation for the enemy to come in.

As the story continues, I did not backslide, but I was not fully committed and was doing my own thing. When my world started falling apart (relationships going south, finances falling apart, and heights of discouragement creeping in, to name a few), I realized that all this started happening because I had run ahead of God and only included Him at a minimal level. God is merciful, and everything truly works together for good. He has a love for us that I can't understand. I believe He allowed my world to fall apart because He saw my destructive behavior and had to get my attention. I had to relinquish control of my life to God; I had to go back to that place of intimacy. It was a real struggle to find that place again, but I had to be persistent, even on the days when I felt horrible and really discouraged and even when it seemed as if the situations were not changing. I was there! You may experience these feelings and much more, but keep on pushing. God is right there with you. Being in that place now where I have regained that intimacy with God, I have said to myself, "Girl, how could you have left the safety of God's arms in the first place? How could you have been so blind?" Now that I am back in this place, everything is not peachy; it's not all butterflies and roses. Trials are still present, but I am navigating life better than I did before, and I just have this peace that is almost scary, if you know what I mean. I was doing my laundry the other day, and I started to reflect on my experiences, and the thought hit me again, *Why don't we just let God?*

Let Him be that coach in the difficult situation. Let Him guide you on how to deal with that difficult person at work, that wayward child, that unsaved husband/wife, that impossible situation. Let Him manage your finances. Let Him show you how to respond in love rather than anger. This is not something that I have placed on paper to sound good; this is real and possible. I have experienced it. I am just encouraged and amazed. I still beat myself up at times, wondering what I was thinking.

I am going to throw this out there. If God has a panoramic view of our lives, as He boldly told us according to His Word in Isaiah 46:10, then He is aware of every single detail of our lives. Yet it seems so hard to let Him help us from day to day. Is the gift of freedom of choice so enticing? Is it the gift of free will that is the obstacle? Is it the need to be in control? Is it a lack of trust? Is His timing too slow? Whatever is happening in our lives right now, whether it is good or bad, we tend to think we only need God when we are going through rough times. Whatever it is, why don't you let God?

Day 25

Lesson: Don't Back Down—Part 1

"If My people who are called by My name will humble themselves, and pray and seek My face, and turn from their wicked ways, then I will hear from heaven, and will forgive their sin and heal their land."
—2 Chronicles 7:14 NKJV

Amid all that is happening in the world today, it is easy to throw in the towel and accept the standards set by the world. We live in a world where there is a constant battle between the forces of God Almighty and those of Satan. Immorality wants to dominate in the form of abortion, murder, alternative lifestyles, incest, prostitution, child abuse, molestation, alterations to the unit of family, alterations to the institution of marriage, broken marriages, and increased divorce rates, to name a few. This was never so because dominion was given to humans long ago in the garden of Eden, and as the redeemed people of God, we are the people who must dominate in the earth, not these immoral ideals.

As God's representatives on earth, we have been called to take a stand for Him. As children of God and citizens of the kingdom, we must take a stand against these things. Let us not be intimidated by the principalities and powers, which are the demonic forces behind the influence of people, world governments, and their policies that promote violation of God's laws. We carry the power and authority to change the course of world events, but the church continues to be silent and very comfortable in most cases. Let us open our mouths and pray so that God can act. We need to make some sacrifices for our beliefs. When we are studying for an exam, our desire is to pass, so we sacrifice sleep, staying awake until the wee hours of the morning to study, ensuring that we not only pass but get an excellent grade. People of God, how can we sleep when these immoral and ungodly acts are happening in our world?

Let us get up out of our comfort zone and battle in prayer. We need to be complaining less and praying more, and this means getting less sleep sometimes. Esther's decision to do something about the Jews' situation changed the course of a decision that was sealed with the king's signet, which once done, could not be changed. Esther aligned herself with the promises of God to Israel, and she moved in faith. She made a petition on behalf of her people, and they were saved. Kingdom people, prayer is petitioning heaven so the angels of God can act on earth. The Word says that we can be confident that once we pray according to God's will, He hears us and grants the petitions we ask of Him. Our prayers are being heard in heaven. We are world changers; we can change legislations and policies across the world that are contrary to God's standards. The believers prayed when Peter was in prison, and as a result, the prison doors that were tightly locked had to open. Paul and Silas in prison … need I say more? Is there anything too hard for God to do?

Day 26

Lesson: Don't Back Down—Part 2

Righteousness exalts a nation, but sin
is a reproach to any people.
—Proverbs 14:34 NKJV

Let us pray with purpose, power, and conviction. God is coming back to judge us. Are we not alarmed? We have become a lukewarm body who profess that we follow Jesus Christ. If we follow Jesus Christ, we must know the power of the Father. Jesus Christ knew the power of His Father, so He spent hours in prayer, and the miraculous did happen. Situations had to change. Will we stand on the sidelines and continue to utter that these are the last days, so these things must happen. These are in fact the last days, and because this is so, it should be of great concern, as we have even less time, and there are a lot of souls to be saved. We have to stand in the face of evil and not only denounce it but exercise our God-given authority over it.

Christians, do we not know that Satan is already defeated? So why are we so timid? Why are we so comfortable? We carry power to defeat the enemy, to defeat any situation that confronts us. The workers of iniquity are not backing down, so why are we? If you are not operating how God says you must, it means you do not believe the Bible, and I make no apologies for this statement. The world and its powers cannot defeat the church or our purpose. The only way they have access to do so is if we continue to operate as people who do not know our God-given identity.

God loves His creation, but He hates sin, and we cannot continue to glorify behaviors that are known violations of God's Word. We are called to stand firm in this battle. We don't know all that it will cost us, but we know that once we stand for God, we can be sure our reward will be exceedingly great. He honors those who honor Him. God does not violate His Word (Psalm 138:2). He honors His Word above His name. Whatever goes against God's Word is wrong and will always be wrong, and whatever is in accordance with God's Word is right and will always be right. "Woe to those who call evil good, and good evil; Who put darkness for light, and light for darkness; who put bitter for sweet, and sweet for bitter" (Isaiah 5:20 NJKV). Do not let Satan or his agents silence or intimidate you because you stand for God. "There is a way that seems right to a man, but its end is the way of death" (Proverbs 16:25 NKJV). Please note it is never too late to repent of any wrong act. God's mercy is continually flowing while we live in the constraints of time. Let us make it right before we face eternity.

To my brethren in Jesus Christ:

Take a stand against the evils in this world. Everything you see happening in violation of God's Word has a demonic influence. Let us be in prayer at all times!

Day 27

Lesson: What Kind of Soil Are You?

Pause for a moment and examine the weight
of this question. Then read the passage.
In Matthew 13, Jesus spoke the parable of the sower
and the different soils. Today we must examine
our lives against the Word. This spoke volumes
to me, and I know it will do the same for you.
Let us examine Matthew 13:1–8 and 18–23.

The Parable of the Sower (Excerpt from the Holy Bible NIV)

That same day Jesus went out of the house and sat by the lake. Such large crowds gathered around him that he got into a boat and sat in it, while all the people stood on the shore. Then he told them many things in parables, saying: "A farmer went out to sow his seed. As he was scattering the seed, some fell along the path, and the birds came and ate it up. Some fell on rocky places, where it did not have much soil. It sprang up quickly, because the soil was shallow. But when the sun came up, the plants were scorched, and they withered because they had no root. Other seed fell among thorns, which grew up and choked the plants. Still other seed fell on good soil, where it produced a crop—a hundred, sixty or thirty times what was sown. Whoever has ears, let them hear."

"Listen then to what the parable of the sower means: When anyone hears the message about the kingdom and does not understand it, the evil one comes and snatches away what was sown in their heart. This is the seed sown along the path. The seed falling on rocky ground refers to someone who hears the word and at once receives it with joy. But since they have no root, they last only a short time. When trouble or persecution comes because of the word, they quickly fall away. The seed falling among the thorns refers to someone who hears the word, but the worries of this life and the deceitfulness of wealth choke the word, making it unfruitful. But the seed falling on good soil refers to someone who hears the word and understands it. This is the one who produces a crop, yielding a hundred, sixty or thirty times what was sown."

Now take a moment to examine your life. Has the Word of God fallen among the wayside, in stony places, among thorns, or is it producing fruit in your life? Jesus reminded us that "He cuts off every branch in me that bears no fruit, while every branch that does bear fruit He prunes so that it will be even more fruitful" (John 15:2 NIV).

What kind of soil are you?

Day 28

Lesson: Reflections

In their hearts humans plan their course,
but the LORD establishes their steps.
—Proverbs 16:9 NIV

So many times, things are happening in our lives, and we blame the devil, but what if it is God allowing things to happen to get our attention? We have to be at the place where we are honest enough to examine ourselves, honest enough to be transparent with others, honest enough with God. We cannot hide anything from God, and He chastens those whom He loves. What if the trial is God's way of getting your attention? I was at a place where things kept happening, and while I knew the enemy was involved, I believed God allowed it for my good, to get my attention and for His glory so that I can share with you. If I had continued down the path I was on, you would not be reading these words today. God is taking me to a new place of maturity in Him, and I am extremely grateful and overwhelmed by His grace. It is amazing how the love of God can change your perspective when you are on a destructive path, scared, feeling inadequate, unlovable, impure, broken, and lost. The love of God is amazing. It has no bounds, and it knows no limits. We are truly blessed to have someone like that in our corner.

Can we ever repay this debt to Him? Never. But for some reason, He keeps holding us together. Let us walk in this love and live according to the purpose He has prepared. There is no task as important as doing what we were made to do. At the end of the day, it is only what we do for Jesus Christ that will count in this life and the next. Let us not let Him down, as He has invested a lot in us. Give the spiritual and physical returns that are due to Him. Be mindful that we can never repay God for all that He has done, but we can live a holy and consecrated life unto Him. I pray your hearts will be blessed and your spirits stirred as you move to the next level in what the Lord has prepared for you. Be honest with yourself and God. Be reminded also that He loves you with an everlasting, boundless, persistent, and pure love. God bless you all, now and forever. Amen and amen. His love was poured out on the cross so that it could be poured out in your life! Say this prayer as you reflect:

Write the story of my heart, Lord. Write the chapter of my outcome. You see me in my imperfections and love me anyhow. There is no standard to gain Your love or acceptance. The love You have for me is mind-blowing. Thanks for loving me. Please direct my steps. Amen.

Day 29

Lesson: Blast Off

For since the beginning of the world, men
have not heard nor perceived by the ear, nor
has the eye seen any God besides You, Who
acts for the one who waits for Him.
—Isaiah 64:4 NKJV

Eye has not seen, nor ear heard, nor have
entered into the heart of man, the things which
God has prepared for those who love Him.
—1 Corinthians 2:9 NKJV

January 4, 2019, marks three years since I joined my current organization in an entirely new field. Each year, we have an event known as Blast Off, where we come together as a team and the CEO shares the objectives for the year with everyone. As we prepared for the 2019 event, I could not help but reflect.

Three years ago on January 4, 2016, I took a bold step, a leap of faith actually. In December 2015, I felt it was time to leave the job I was offered after my layoff at work. I left even though I knew my contract would have been renewed based on my work ethic. I took a new job on January 4, 2016, where I was offered a six-month contract as a teller, filling in for someone who was on maternity leave. I did not know what would happen thereafter. At first, it was like the new job made no sense. Financially, I would be spending more, as it would require me traveling a greater distance—approximately one hour, compared to the one I left, which was like ten minutes from home. At first, I found every reason why I could not take it. Furthermore, my good friend and I spoke about it, and we both agreed it made no sense. I made up my mind to turn down the offer, and I heard the voice of the Holy Spirit say, "Take the job." I picked up the phone and called my friend to tell her I had changed my mind about taking the job. To my surprise, she replied that she was about to call back to tell me to take it.

I tendered my resignation and started my journey at the new job as a bank teller. I must tell you I had previously worked as a bank teller, and it was not something I was fond of. There is nothing wrong with being a teller, but each person has their passion, and it wasn't mine. I, however, did the job to the best of my ability and with zeal, so you couldn't tell it was not my thing. We should always work as unto God because we never know who is watching, and most importantly, God is watching. Since I moved to this organization, I have had obstacles, but God has been awesome. In the space of three years, I became permanent and have been promoted three times. I do not share this to boast or gloat; I am just showing how God works. People who saw me moving into these positions would joke and say, "I wonder which new position you will be in next week." Let me tell you this: when God favors you, absolutely nothing can stop you but *you*. Is there anything too hard for God to do?

God doesn't do safe. He is radical. You cannot let fear stop you. It is necessary to get out of your comfort zone to accomplish what He has planned. Even after my previous experiences, I am reluctant sometimes, but I have made a decision that as long as the Lord is with me and goes before me, then I must act in obedience and do what He says. I didn't have the resources figured out to begin publishing, and I am someone who likes to have it all figured out. I made the decision to take a leap of faith. Faith requires stepping out even when we can't see the end from the beginning. God revealed to me that if I am able to do it on my own, then it is not faith; that is called being self-sufficient. Don't let anything stop you from stepping into what He has prepared for you. Eyes have not seen and ears have not heard, neither has it entered into the hearts of humankind the things God has prepared for those who love Him, for those who seek to do His will and honor His name (paraphrasing).

As I attended the annual Blast Off event, I was reminded of God's love. I am just in awe of where God has taken me, where we are going, what He will do, and what we will together. Together we are unstoppable. Together we are unshakeable, and the term *blast off* has taken on a whole new meaning. There is so much more to do and so much more to accomplish. Through this journey, I have also come to a place where I am learning to appreciate everything in my life—the good, bad, and the indifferent—because those experiences are working for my good. I realize that I am in that season again where God is about to do something radical, and I am praying, listening, waiting, and anticipating.

Today, get out of the safe mind-set, the calculated mind-set, the "I won't go if I don't have it all figured out" mind-set. God has got you. God has got you! You will never know until you go. As I reflect, I give God thanks!

Day 30

Lesson: The Place of Surrender

And do not be conformed to this world, but
be transformed by the renewing of your
mind, that you may prove what is that good
and acceptable and perfect will of God.
—Romans 12:2 NKJV

Transform your mind to know God's will, and He will reveal same to you. He promised He would (paraphrased).

For some time now, my spirit has been restless. I have been searching to get clarity about God's will and my purpose. It is amazing how the Holy Spirit works. I decided to reread a book I bought years ago. This book, though I had encountered it before, confirmed again what I felt in my spirit years ago but somehow laid aside because I was busy chasing and finding fulfillment in the things of the world. Anything by Jennie Allen really confirmed what I was feeling, and the Lord used it to minister to me. (Keep doing the great work of the Lord, Jennie.) I prayed my anything prayer because I was at a place where I needed more. My life is bigger than me. I was honest with God. I was feeling afraid because I didn't know where being surrendered would take me, and I just associated it with suffering like many others. I wanted to be honest with God, so I laid it all out about how I felt, and He already knew that anyway. Deep down, I am hoping this will be an amazing adventure, but whatever comes, by God's grace I will get through it.

I am different, so are you, and it is okay to be different. Not superior different, but I have a desire for more. There have been times in my life when I felt like God was deliberately withholding good things from me, things that I clearly thought were mine—promotions at work I was qualified for, relationships, material things, and so on. In reflecting now, I understand. He has bigger desires for me, and my motives were wrong. You do not get what you ask for because you ask amiss (see James 4). My motive for asking God has always been for my outcome because I felt entitled. I felt I was not a perfect Christian but a good one, so God should give me my desires. I felt like He should bless me, and at times I got frustrated because I felt He was holding out on me. At times I have questioned whether this is real, and what is the sense of being a Christian? Maybe I was better off in the world. People who have not yet given their hearts to God and are living how they please, and even those who don't believe in Him at all, seem to be accomplishing what they want, and I was serving God, and it seemed liked I was getting nowhere. I really felt like God was being unfair to me, and how could He love me but withhold things from me?

I even went as far as comparing my relationship with God to that of my relationship with my mother. God said in His Word that if our earthly father gives good gifts, He gives even greater/ better gifts. I was like, "God, when I want something and my mother can afford to help me, she does. Why is it that You, who are indeed real and the maker of the universe, do not give me the things I desire?" I even surmised that what I was asking for was not unreasonable or over the top. But after all this wrestling, I realized that my desires were selfish, and I was praying for the things that gave me pleasure rather than those that would truly glorify God.

I am always praying about promotions, relationships, and material accomplishments, which is not bad, but I was created for so much more. There is a longing to dream beyond those things, to make a marked difference for His kingdom. We place so much emphasis on these things, and if we reach a particular age and have not accomplished these things, we start to panic. We have become fixated on the temporal rather than the eternal. I have spent so much time and energy figuring how to get these things when God is calling me to greater. If you never get these things in life, it shouldn't matter, because at the end of this life, they will not matter. Only what you do for God will truly count. Life is more than eating, drinking, and accolades. It is okay to be at a specific age and to not have accomplished these things; your focus should be on seeking His kingdom above all. Jesus had none of these, yet he accomplished so much. He laid claim to nothing in this world, only doing the will of His Father, who sent Him. Satan captures our hearts through the things of this world, but God has a greater plan. Remember—we are His hands and feet, so we should go. We must go.

I am now at a place waiting to see what God will do with a heart that is surrendered, that will love Him above all else and that will trust Him completely. I am scared that this might mean suffering. Deep down, I want it to be a case where He uses me to make a real difference, a case where others will start seeing the real Him without me having to suffer through loss or sickness. But whatever the outcome, as long as it is a part of the story that He wrote for me, according to Psalm 139, it is okay because good will come. If we are truly obedient, we cannot choose the path or method He uses to advance His kingdom through us. He has a panoramic view, and He loves you and me.

Today, I am praying anything, Lord, because I am tired of going around in circles. I want to do what I am here for. Every manufacturer creates a product to achieve a specific outcome, so God created us to achieve a specific outcome. My deepest desire is to live and accomplish the purpose I was created for through the help of the Holy Spirit. When we have amassed wealth, accolades, possessions, and family, we are still not satisfied. This is so because we were made for so much more!

> For to me to live is Christ and to die is gain. (Philippians 1:21 NKJV)

> Yet indeed I also count all things loss for the excellence of the knowledge of Christ Jesus my Lord, for whom I have suffered the loss of all things, and count them as rubbish, that I may gain Christ. (Philippians 3:8 NKJV)

Day 31

Lesson: A Grateful Heart

In everything give thanks; for this is the
will of God in Christ Jesus for you.
—1 Thessalonians 5:18 NKJV

I had a motor vehicle accident, and a few hours prior, I was in deep dialogue with God, so when it happened, I was mad at God. The accident made no sense, and I knew He had the power to prevent it. I was shaken. I cried and asked Him why He allowed it to happen. I was doing what I was supposed to do, and the person came in my path, and even though I felt I did everything in my power to avoid the accident, it still happened. I remember that evening when I returned home, I was in a daze. I was standing in my bathroom, and I started to cry, and this turned to laughter. I was doing both at the same time. My heart was overwhelmed at all that could and had transpired. My first reaction was to be mad, not thankful that no one received any serious injuries.

I could not make sense of anything, and that is when He spoke these words to me. I heard the gentle whisper of the voice of the Holy Spirit telling me, "God's got you." He reminded me that in God's kingdom, no experience is wasted. The enemy thought he was putting Joseph in a pit, but God was preparing him for the palace. There is absolutely nothing too hard for God to do. Remember—God told Paul that chains awaited him, but Paul didn't back down. He preferred to suffer for Christ's sake than to think about his own life. God is powerful, able, and sovereign. He has not given us a spirit of fear but of power, love, and a sound mind. And we know all things work together for the good of those who love God and are called according to His purpose. Do you love God? No experience is wasted. Trust the process. He is willing and working together everything that pertains to His will and purpose for our lives.

Remain thankful with a heart of gratitude, as the situation could be much worse. He will give you the grace to handle whatever you are faced with. It may be hard, painful, and frustrating, but in everything give thanks. I now see God's goodness through this accident, and I can't help but give Him praise and express gratitude for all He has done. Life is what you make it, and I plan to make mine awesome!

Week 4

Action Plan

Identify the areas in your life that you
need to work on in accordance with the
material that was covered in week 4.

Reflect, Resolve, and Move Forward
Turn your eyes upon Jesus.
Look fully in His wonderful face,
And the things of earth will grow strangely dim
In the light of His glory and grace.

Finding Jesus
The Way to Salvation

I am the way, the truth, and the life.

> Jesus said to him, "I am the way, the truth, and the life. No one comes to the Father except through Me." (John 14:6 NKJV)

For God so loved the world.

> For God so loved the world that He gave His only begotten Son, that whoever believes in Him should not perish but have everlasting life. (John 3:16 NKJV)

Today you are granted the gift of everlasting life.

> But if serving the Lord seems undesirable to you, then choose for yourselves this day whom you will serve, whether the gods your ancestors served beyond the Euphrates, or the gods of the Amorites, in whose land you are living. But as for me and my household, we will serve the Lord. (Joshua 24:15 NIV)

Pray the prayer below to receive Jesus as your personal Lord and Savior:

Dear Lord, I thank You for who You are. I thank You for the gift of life that is everlasting and abundant. I believe Jesus died for my sins, past, present, and future. He died and rose on the third day that I might have new life. I acknowledge that I am a sinner in need of a Savior. I humbly bow and ask Your forgiveness for all I have done. I now invite You to come into my heart and every area of my life. In Jesus's name I pray. Amen.

> Likewise, I say to you, there is joy in the presence
> of the angels of God over one sinner who repents.
> (Luke 15:10 NKJV)

Now that you have accepted Jesus Christ as your personal Lord and Savior, please find a Bible-believing church to attend so that you will continue to grow in the Lord.

Send an email to Shamika.D.Hamilton@gmail. We would love to hear from you about how this devotional has impacted your life.

About the Author

Shamika D. Hamilton is passionate about developing others and helping them to find their God-ordained purpose. She is a youth leader, volunteer, and mentor who has served in several leadership capacities. Hamilton enjoys being involved in ministry that is focused on empowering young adults and children. She lives in Jamaica. This is her first book.

Printed in the United States
By Bookmasters